This journal belongs to:

_____

Creator Being

"My intention is to be with you as you expand your ability to **consciously** *manifest with this journal." - Miley*

Table of Contents

WHO ARE LISA, ELIZABETH AND MILEY?

FROM LISA:

In December 2006, my husband Dene and I adopted an adult dog named Miley. She was part of our family until she crossed over in December 2020. Miley came into our lives when we had recently lost our previous dog to cancer. We were so devastated by that loss that we did not believe the emptiness we felt would ever disappear. Miley burst into our reality with her vibrant energy and unique personality, changing everything for us. She was larger than life; her presence immediately filled the house and our hearts.

After fourteen incredible years, our time with her was coming to an end. A chance encounter connected us to Elizabeth Long on the morning of Miley's last day with us.

Even as Miley was still with us as a dog, both Dene and I had begun to expand our consciousness just by interacting with her in our daily lives. Once she crossed over, we began to communicate with her through Elizabeth. She was then revealed as a complex Multidimensional Being, accelerating our expansion. We started to see the Universe from a different perspective and began to understand that things were not always what we had been taught.

Dene and I had already been exploring the processes of Manifestation and The Law of Attraction before our interactions with Miley through Elizabeth. Very early on in our sessions, Miley stepped into the role of our guide and teacher, and we were exposed to a more nuanced view of these concepts. Miley began to instruct us on how to be more successful in **conscious** manifestation. Eventually, it occurred to us to ask her to create an "instruction manual" for us to share that could work for anyone. This journal is a result of that request.

If you want to know more about our story and read the transcripts of Miley's communication sessions with us where she reveals more of her wisdom and beautiful heart, our book "Miley Speaks" will be available shortly for that.

FROM ELIZABETH:

ny human who is interested and who can find a quiet space within, can learn to talk to animals ith practice equivalent to the effort it takes to master a sport or musical instrument.

any of us are born with this innate gift, and gradually relinquish it as the pressure to fit in with hers takes over as we move into adulthood. I was lucky; I chose art as a profession, which only xpanded this world I'd enjoyed as a child. But I have taught many adults to reach deeply into what ey used to know and find that ability to connect, and to understand what animals are feeling and inking. One thing I emphasize is that animals have an incredibly wide range of ability and vareness, with varying spiritual knowiedge and capacity. Talking with animals shows me how milar we humans are to one another.

word about translation: Animals flow energy as vibrational frequencies which we as humans anslate into human language as words. How that happens is mysterious even for those of us who ive experienced this process for decades. What I can tell you about it is that the words and essages form in my mind within a rhythm similar to music. Animals also send visual images, and ill mix these with the energy that gets translated into words. So many times the written result is a anscript with slightly odd punctuation - that's the rhythm of their vibrational frequency. They ause, I use a comma to indicate that. They send an image, I describe it in parentheses. But the sult is also a living manuscript, which means that Miley's words in this book are imbued with her nergy signature. When you read them, you are connected to her heart. Miley notices you as an dividual, and anytime you re-read her words, she may slightly shift the message for you to match ho you are becoming. You'll get it. You'll know something is happening and you are beginning to change energy and messages with animals as well at a very basic level.

ow does Miley know about all this stuff?

iley accesses my memory banks as a library to pull from energetically, using my extensive nowledge of metaphysical, creative and spiritual studies in order to express herself. If I don't have me knowledge of what she wants to talk about, I can only describe it peripherally. Through other animal communicator Miley's messages would have the same feel and essence, but the ords, text etc. would likely be very different, based on that person's library of knowledge.

; a function of being in spirit, she also gathers and relays information from a variety of spiritual urces: Archangels, Teachers of Light, Creator Beings, the Fae and more. Guides for Lisa, Dene and e also participate.

iley serves as narrator, teacher, guide and nurturer in this book. She knows who you are. She ctated almost every single word here, giving Lisa and I a little bit of editing freedom at certain ints. Her energy flows through the pages like a song, and as you begin to let that song vibrate rough you, she can serve as a portal for you in connecting to your own guides and teachers. This cilitates your ability to create your own reality with them. Miley lives in the stars and you can join er there.

FROM MILEY:

I am a Being. I am a spirit, who recently enjoyed an experience on Earth as a dog. I am a spiritual guide dog, and am continuing to help humanity beyond my life supporting my humans.

I am a Guide, who loved commandeering my humans, and wished to continue even as my physical body was laid to rest.

My mission here is to help you grow and change through Consciousness Expansion. This will help shift a portion of human consciousness into a higher vibrational frequency. You are becoming part of that shift simply by having fun and being successful. This desire was born out of my love and devotion to Lisa and Dene, and now I am extending my nurturing to you.

There is really no need for any qualification other than this desire coupled with wisdom, which becomes self-evident through the love emanating from what you as readers will find in your hearts when you connect with me there. I invite you into the beauty of my heart, aligning as Lisa and Dene's did.

I intend to show you who I am, rather than simply tell you about myself. You will discover more about me in the daily quotes and messages from me. Look for who I am between the lines.

WHAT MAKES THIS JOURNAL DIFFERENT?

s a living packet of energy that helps humans align with a higher vibrational frequency. You are t alone in these pages, ever, unless you wish to be. You turn this energy on each time you open s book, or even look into my eyes.

ill be nurturing each of you, as your guide in this process. Your own guides will begin to join me d increase their connection to you.

m imbuing a palpable sense of nurturing joy into these pages. If you are not having fun in this ocess, then please take a moment to adjust your heart connection to me and your guides. Simply quiet and intend this. If you are enjoying yourself here in this manual, you are aligned.

arning to manifest is not so much via instruction as it is a process of discovery. It is unique to ch of you. However, there are some common guidelines that you have probably heard that I will uch on as well. My focus here is to help you find how success works uniquely for you.

derstand that you can be excited about becoming more successful in creating your reality, but it ly takes one failure to spoil the container of creation - your cauldron. This happens when your sonance drops and you mix creating from fear into your desires, for example: "I'm afraid this n't work for me, and I'll fail (again)."

at is somewhat how the fear of failure feels to humans, and I especially want to create this anifesting success manual for those who have struggled. The struggle energy kills creating. So it is t so much that the human fails, as it is simply that struggle seeps into the cauldron and spoils the up. Joy and fun insulate you from struggle.

any manifestation books instruct from a mental level. My aim here is merged with the desires of ur guides. We wish to induce a joyous, excited state of being into the pages so that it becomes mething you can't help but slide into. But you must join us there from your own heart, and allow urself to let go as you put one foot down this slippery slope that leads to an elevated way of living.

e are going deeper into how reality creation works from a heartspace. That is where you will sorb it rather than learn it, which is a surprisingly easier way of manifesting. Your delight in periencing that will fuel greater manifesting capabilities. Your primary instruction as you proceed ough these 30 days, is to expand into your heart into that place of joy and delight.

is process will allow you to consciously radiate more feelings of happiness and well-being that pport your manifestation success, but you must intend it! You are creating an infinite feedback op that expands and becomes a powerful manifesting circuit as you develop it over time.

(continued on next page)

This is both a how-to manual and a journal of co-creation between me and you. Very few wish to do this alone. Sharing success is a large part of being successful, so talk to me in your heartspace - tell me about your successes. I am listening.

I do not want to interrupt your own process of how you already manifest or how you already connect with your own guides or Beings such as me. This journal is an open book for discovery with me and others, as much or as little as you wish to engage in co-creation. Protect and nurture your own daily manifestation process as you grow it during these 30 days. It's yours, and you will know it more intimately if you do not share it with others until it bears fruit.

Your own guides and I are available here to support and help you expand your ideas and desires. We will never criticize you or tell you you're wrong, because you aren't. New ideas develop and change. A caterpillar is not wrong even though it transforms completely when it becomes a butterfly.

What do you wish to manifest?

You may already know what you want, and within these pages you can allow that to grow.

To start: Imagine what you want to create, visualize a rough outline of an image that shows or symbolizes that, and allow your own guides to fill in the outline for you. Use your intuition to merge your creative energy with universal knowledge this way.

What are these universal feedback messages?

Repeating numbers, colors, images and interactive experiences are signs. You notice the time, and it's 11:11, or 3:33; or you're driving and you see that the license plate on the car in front of you matches some of your own personal numbers. When you pay more attention to what you used to think of as coincidences, your personal universal feedback language will grow and develop into more complex and complete pieces of information and knowledge.

Think about what you want often throughout your day, stop and take a moment to use this process of seeing the visual outline of it, and then let go. Your own guides and I will pick up the process, and weave the light of the center of the Universe into what you desire, and flow feedback to you by tomorrow. Let go, and then look for it.

Be patient. The Universe also speaks to you in both night and daydreams, through the words of strangers and the acts of your own animal companions. Look into their eyes for wisdom that is yours, as well. How feedback is presented to you is as unlimited as your imagination.

These daily hits of support from the Universe also let you know 'It's working!', and reinforce the manifestation process by anchoring a template of a feeling of success inside you.

MY MANIFESTING INTENTIONS

What do you want to create? What has been on your mind for a long time, and what just popped into your head now that you wish to manifest in your life?

"As I begin this journey, these are some of the things that I wish to manifest..."

_____

_____

_____

_____

_____

_____

_____

There are many ways to immerse yourself in 3 6 9 manifesting energy, and one way is to move your own creativity into the shape that depicts the number in human consciousness. Here are some examples of how you can be creative and merge your own consciousness from a highly creative state with the numbers' visual symbol. You can even color these in, and add them anywhere you feel like in this journal - your own versions of 3 6 9 images. Have fun as you own these numbers through infusing your preferences.

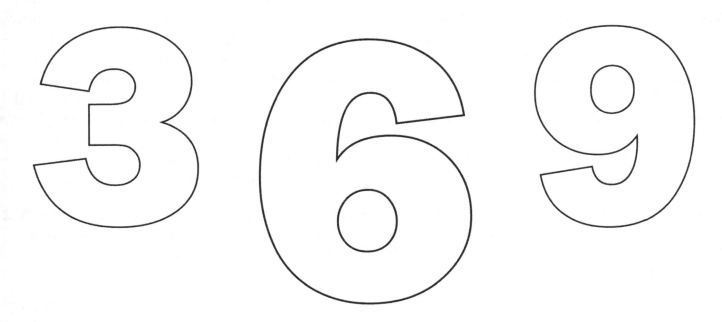

The Magic of 3 6 9

There is a great deal of magic in the numbers 3, 6 and 9, from many human perspectives. These numbers and the geometrics that express variations of them resonate through your vast universe, independent of human perspective. Much creative energy lies in wait between these two statements and is available for creative use even if you adopt only the most basic concepts as a tool for manifesting your reality. You don't have to know or understand details to benefit from their magic. Many who work with 3, 6, 9 energy suggest specific instructions a certain number of times per day. I work with alignment, and if you work with your manual here once a day, you will maintain your alignment for at least 24 hours. Relax, and enjoy your day.

I will tell you some things about these numbers for you to simply enjoy and begin to resonate with. Open your heart, and allow your own vibrational frequency to radiate and align with these numbers as you consider them in your creative studio here. Wait until you feel this before you go forward.

3 is the number of creativity. All energy must have a geometric form in order to become physical, the triangle is the most stable geometry. I suggest simply visualizing a triangle as you list your 3 things you desire to create.

6 is the number of partnerships. When your own energy, especially love, is reflected back to you from another, you are experiencing an act of co-creation. So if you bring a reflection of who you are from any other Being into your creative studio, then you are adding a frequency loop.

How does this work? Practice giving and receiving. You can send and receive messages from me, as another Being. When you are practicing the 6 things you intend to nurture your Self with during your day, imagine running an infinity loop from your heart to another: Another human or animal, Source energy in the Universe, or just me or one of your guides. You are not alone, ever. Sit in this infinity loop and allow the energy of love from your own heart to flow out, and return carrying more nurturing and love to you.

9 is a spiritual access point. Here is where you can both send and receive energy. At a very basic but powerful level in this Phase One journal, we will focus on the natural property of ebb and flow that correlates with using frequency or sound to create. For example, you can feel and even hear the magic in your favorite song when an emotion is placed on top of a vibrational frequency. And this works whether it is an audible sound vibration or not. How much fun can you have with this? Singing or listening to a song is a successful alignment with a frequency. You can make music and that is very powerful. But all you have to do at a basic level to use this in your manifestations, is use your voice: Talk, sing, tone, scream, yell, shout. What are you feeling, what are you thinking and what are you intending while doing that? For our Phase One work, simply think about these questions as you play with your voice or other sound waves. There is much more, of course.

You can do fewer things to nurture yourself if you are having more fun, for the same creative effect. In an energy of fun, your body is supported in adjusting, rebalancing. The exhilaration of having fun, of joy, is more powerful than any drug or healing process. You cannot overdose on fun or become addicted to it, either.

There is magic in the telling. That's the number 9, in action. There is much more, but get started at this basic level and become more aware of your own power as you enjoy infinite variations of these processes. Be creative. Do what you want to do.

MANIFESTING

tention is the one and only direct manifestation tool that I suggest you use in this Phase One
urnal. Everything else I will discuss here is about alignment: Raising your own vibrational
quency to support that intention, and creating a reception for your creation to land in the
ghest level of joy that you can hold. You are creating the energy of the backdrop of your reality -
e landing strip. Here you can see how applying the law of attraction is interwoven: Create the best
tting for what you want, and let it come to you as you practice your daily 3 intentions, your 6 acts
nurturing your own Self, and your 9 joyous celebrations of having fun and enjoying your life.

anifesting is a process of how reality creation works. The advantage of working with our 3 6 9
anual is that we are going directly deeper into that from a broader base that includes
nsciousness Expansion. Keeping it simple and avoiding overly mental chatter will allow a
rprisingly more effective way of actually manifesting, which you will be delighted to discover. And
at delight will fuel greater manifesting capabilities. Delight is fertilizer for creating realities, you
e.

ould like to offer you some specific suggestions concerning your own reality creation
ckground and context for expanding your manifesting.

st, get comfortable and align with the concept of allowing as an energy. Do not separate
iritual and/or personal growth from manifesting. They are all intertwined within the same
ocess of reality creation. Whether you intend to or not, you create all of your reality within the
o methods of reality creation: Allowing and/or creating, mostly in co-creation with others.

t at first you are not conscious of this, and that is what brings you to think from a state of
paration, so that only occasionally will you try to focus on 'manifesting' something. This is like
nking, "I will try to practice breathing, an in-breath today: I will try to see if I can create
eathing." Yet you know you breathe every minute of your life. This journal is not for intermittent
anifesting; it is for helping you to become conscious of everything that you already manifest, and
choring that into your own awareness by focusing on your 3, 6 and 9 named daily intentions and
sires. Become comfortable with your creations that are already working and accept your own
ccesses. That alignment is your launchpad, your platform for creating more of what you
nsciously desire in your life through evolving your 3 6 9 daily entries.

THE LAW OF ATTRACTION

The Law of Attraction has been discussed by many and is quite simple, but few humans understand or discuss it in its entirety. I would like to endeavor to do that, in as few words as possible in order to allow you to simply adjust how you understand and use it so that it might work more effectively for you.

There are two parts: **How you already use it, and how you might wish to use it more effectively.**

When the law of attraction is interpreted incompletely from one perspective, some humans interpret it too simply and blame themselves when it 'does not work'. In actuality it is working and they simply do not understand that 5% of their attention is on creating what they want consciously, while 95% of their unconscious attention remains on what they fear. That is the unconscious underbelly of your fears creating 95% of your reality.

If you as a human are not consciously in charge of your emotions and thoughts, then you are not able to direct them towards what you want to create. However they do not just sit quietly on the sidelines. Those energies within you continue to generate elements of your reality. So until you work to become aware of all your thoughts and feelings on all levels: Conscious, semi-conscious, subconscious and unconscious; you are not able to pull together all of your reality-generating energies into one focus, which is what you want to create.

I suggest working from a base level to expand your awareness of what you are already thinking and feeling on all levels, rather than layer a short meditation on top of all of these subterranean processes. This is the importance of expanding your consciousness in order to use what you know more effectively.

This, my dearest students, is a big project. Begin to become gradually aware of thoughts you are running in the background, or an anxiety just beneath your skin that has been there so long it feels normal to you now. Just start with this. Your guides and I will expand our abilities to help you sort these out in the next phase of journaling. You can begin your journey of becoming more conscious of your reality creating process for now, and understand that if you attract what you do not want, in fact what you fear; well, now you know where it is coming from. The Law of Attraction works, and works best when you learn how to hone your craft in using it.

FROM LISA:

ver the last several years, my unexpected journey with Miley has taught me that she is incredibly ise. Only good things happen when I am smart enough to follow her advice.

ere is an excellent example of what I have learned from Miley: Today is a great day because I am tting my intention for it to be so. Then magically, it is a great day, no matter what happens. And nce I choose to be happy each day, then I am happy, regardless of what is going on around me.

you follow her instructions, don't overthink it, and get out of your head space and into your heart ace, (something I have to continuously work on and remind myself to do - it's not always easy and n not always successful - but when I am successful I celebrate it); then good things will happen to u too.

me of the drawings are simple and others have more detail. Don't be intimated if you are not in e habit of drawing or coloring. This is not an art contest and no one is judging you. Miley has a rpose for each of you with these exercises, and the process will be different for everyone. Do at feels right for you, and it will be exactly what you are meant to be doing.

iley, Elizabeth and I have co-created this journal not just for you, but also for ourselves. Elizabeth d I are using it every day, and are excited to see what the universe brings next. We hope you njoy exploring your Creation Studio as much as we have enjoyed designing it.

FROM ELIZABETH:

most every time I sat down to write or edit this journal with Miley, I had some ideas of what she ight say, but she always had even better ideas! Even after talking to animals all these years, I am ten shocked by their wisdom, seemingly out of nowhere. But clearly it comes from somewhere, d that begins with the unconditional love they are uniquely able to share with us.

iley has some tough love to offer at times, as well as a gentleness that will bring tears to my eyes hen she leans in. I've learned to absorb all of this best by leaving a side door open - let it seep into ur life. Look for the universal feedback. That's my best suggestion for allowing your own platform 3 6 9 to emerge as a process. For example, just decide to let yourself notice all the ways you ready do nurture yourself; those can be one of your 6 daily nurturing expressions, and you can list several times a day if that makes your heart sing. We want your heart to sing - that is what this urnal is about: Creating the backdrop for the magic of 3 6 9 to run in your life like an automatic ogram. Your conscious job is to maintain your elevated mental and emotional states.

ith Miley's tutoring through these pages, your current reality will morph into what you want, in a ry similar manner to how the rhythm of a song emerges out of the repeating chorus and verse ructure. Science says we're all made of numbers. Our conscious mind tells us this is crazy. Miley is ere to tell us how to bridge the gap.

HOW TO RECEIVE MESSAGES FROM MILEY AND YOUR OWN GUIDES

Look into my eyes in the photo. Then look away or close your eyes and begin to imagine. Visualize the outline of the image of me, and allow me to fill in the outline drawing. You may see or sense this, or simply feel it in your heart.

This instruction is how my friend Elizabeth shows students how to connect with Beings who do not speak human languages, and I am using this same method here in teaching you to connect with me in order to co-create. The quickest and easiest way to step into the stream of communication is through the presence of your own heart. You can use this process to communicate with me, and as you practice, develop it in your own way. Your own guides will begin to step into this stream with us.

So start with me, and follow the process above. Look into my eyes using the photo of me that speaks to your heart most. Allow your heart to connect, and close your eyes while you begin to imagine. You can choose the drawings or the photos. Relax, our connection is through your heart via a happy warm feeling.

If you feel uncomfortable in any way, that is simply the fear of failure that we are here to help you avoid. Give it to me - send it to me, and wrap yourself in a sky blue feeling of happiness, and relax. Then stop, go about your day, and allow me to initiate a connection with you when you are enjoying your day.

That is your primary instruction throughout this process: Enjoy your day. I serve as a guide and as a doorway to your own guides. For fun, see if you can sense messages from your own guides. For fun! Imagine you can sense it as a ping notification on your phone. Record whatever you sense or even think you sense, here, in your journal. Writing it down helps make it real.

HOW TO USE THIS JOURNAL

earning to manifest is more a process of discovery than instruction, then this journal's highest
e is to first discover within yourself what you already know about manifesting. All processes of
arning here will lead to that, so indulge yourself freely and creatively within the pages. There is no
ht or wrong way; there is only your way and that is what you are here to discover more about.

e have created a structure to support your **wild imagination**, so bring it to the table when you sit
wn daily to explore within the process. Your **wild imagination** is your most valuable asset as a
man being; everything else we teach is here for crafting what you want with that tool.

e instructions on each journaling page create the structure. Follow them. Here in the how-to
ction; we are mostly helping you move into crafting with your imagination within that structure.

First: In Your Daily Practice

a daily basis, you will be creating your 3 6 9 entries, connecting with me as you read and absorb
daily message into your heartspace where I will join you with subtle guidance. It will take some
actice to find how you hear me best. Do not overtly focus on it; let it come to you in your own
ique way.

e other part of your daily entries are the exercises on the drawing pages. These are created by
, for you, to complete each day. They will help you creatively move into a magical mindset in
ur heartspace.

ur daily entries are where you allow yourself to become more and more of who you truly are,
pported by me and your guides. Look at me as the portal, as your own guides begin to amplify
eir messages to you here as well. Relax, and understand that this is a daily practice that will grow
ur ability to connect and hear them more clearly over time.

ere is a simple structure within the fractals and rhythm of the 3 6 9 intentions, that acts as a
rturing embrace to hold your own process in alignment within your highest and best interest.

Second: Consider how you as a human recognize
and absorb daily universal feedback

is journal is a place to document that process. You see, as you begin to connect with the Universe
rough this feedback process more consciously, you will first find glimpses of feedback as the
iverse pokes holes in your daily backdrop of reality, allowing light to stream in. Look for these
nals and note them in the reflection spaces.

(continued on next page)

Third: Take the messages into your heart

Look at your messages that you have recorded in your creation studio, and allow whatever you find to integrate into your heart. That means you must get into your heartspace first. Close your eyes and move your focus there. Ask me to help if you freeze - just look into my eyes, and remember how much animals have loved you unconditionally.

Intend to let all the universal feedback you have picked up during the day or previous day, settle into your heart. That's it, you're done. Do not question it.

Now: Ground your Universal Feedback

This is simple, short but important: Trust. This means immerse yourself in the experience. Keep dreaming and hold your energy high throughout your day.

Q&A between Lisa and Miley after Lisa started using the journal
(as translated by Elizabeth)

E: "If time is a factor is it ok to do the affirmation page first and then later do the drawing page when I have more time to spend on it?"

M: Absolutely! There is no right or wrong way to use the journal. You are discovering it is a highly individual experience, very different for each human, based on their history and unique makeup. And time does not have to enter into this - each set of pages can be approached as the student ha an inclination to. You see, you will automatically assume processes that are different for each of you. Lisa, your assumption of a way to work with this book is based on your sense of order. That is your way of doing things that is most comfortable to you.

Each person's sense of order is different, so I want to structure the process in an open way that accommodates and validates all senses of order. I wish to develop a sense of joy, excitement and experimentalism within each person's sense of comfort. Reality is created most fluidly for each person using their own innate processes comfortably. This journal is me, setting a table, for each o you to sit down and enjoy whatever you'd like to order off the menu. The universal kitchen can prepare any meal you can imagine.

E: "And also, what if I am listing my 9 things I will do for fun and then I'm stumped? Can I walk awa from it and then come back to it later, or do I need to concentrate and finish it all at once?"

M: Your guideline is to do what's comfortable for you and it can be different every time. This is an intimate process, which means what happens on the pages and in the process, is not for anyone but the student and me. As long as their hearts are one with the process and they are engaged, they can skip days or integrate it into other processes, as long as they STAY ENGAGED. It should simply become part of each person, to use in a way that they have no variance with. Do you understand that part? No variance means oneness, a fifth dimensional concept, you can't do it wrong as long as you are engaged with love.

FINAL INSTRUCTIONS FROM MILEY

y dear students, come closer, now. Here is a place where I wish to whisper in your ear, to help you
e in as much of a state of ease as you can manage, as you open your heart to both me and your
wn creative process.

hen you go to your daily page, do not feel rushed. Instead pause, and allow yourself to
ander....across the page. I would like for you to slow down, and not for 5 minutes only to speed
ack up again. Pace yourself. In spending some time creating what you want, you will allow yourself
 drop into a deeper level when you sit with the pages.

olor some of the fractals, copy them by hand, and elaborate - add more to them. Do this on the
ages, so that you can get a sense of how this book feels to YOU, how it flows for YOU. Let yourself
 into an easy meditation, after you note what you want to create: Your 3 6 9 intentions. Yes, so
any of you want to get these done and you are very good at getting things done. It is important
at you are allowing yourself to live the process enough so that it will change you. Slow down. Sit.
editate or simply relax and dream. Record notes with the exercises. Some of you are more
omfortable making visual notes, please do not hesitate to be yourself.

here is no pressure to do this a certain way, no right or wrong. You might ask if it is okay to list
omething really special to you more than once. And you might push that to an extreme: What if
our version of self nurturing is to eat pistachio ice cream six times in one day? Of course you can
o that, but consider within the wisdom of your own heart if that is a good idea. Will it get me what I
ant? I want a very expensive dress....what if you create that dress, after a month of eating
istachio ice cream 6 times a day? You have free will, an open heart and more wisdom than you
ealize. Use all of these tools of creation.

onfusion can be part of your reality creation process, or not. If you can accept yourself, then also
ccept that opening up your own treasure chest of processes and tools that you already use to
anifest could be slightly disruptive. You can then choose to enjoy the ride through your own
onsciousness expanding into a larger place, where thoughts and feelings that are not conducive
or creating what you want can leave. You simply allow them to release, and let new thoughts and
eelings that you are consciously choosing, to settle into a comfortable alignment with little
isruption.

ealize that the physical sensation of a wild carnival ride is very similar to getting dumped off your
urfboard by a rogue wave. One is within a context of excitement and expectations of fun, the
ther is within a context of disruption, and possibly even fear. Your choice of how to experience
ny process is important, and has the greatest impact on the results.

use intentions as reality creation tools in this journal rather than affirmations, because they are
ore effective and less confusing to your subconscious. Like you, I want results, for you.

This is a fractal called a Mandelbrot, which is a complex reality generating machine. You can begin to play with it and absorb some of its functionality here by simply having fun with it. Imagine that if you re-draw it or color it in, it will begin to support YOUR reality creation.

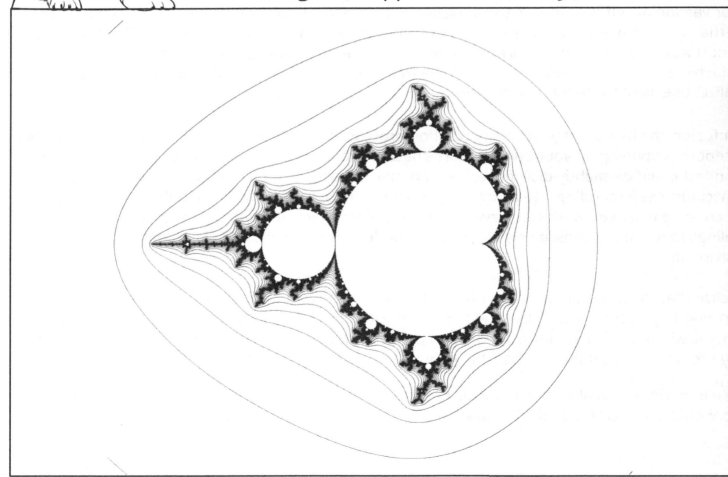

You are the originator and creator of your reality.

I am starting today with...
3 Things My Heart Wants To Manifest:

1._____
2._____
3._____

6 Things I Will Do For Self-Care Today.

1._____
2._____
3._____
4._____
5._____
6._____

9 Things I Will Do For Fun Today.

1._____
2._____
3._____
4._____
5._____
6._____
7._____
8._____
9._____

Notes:

Date: _____

REFLECTIONS:

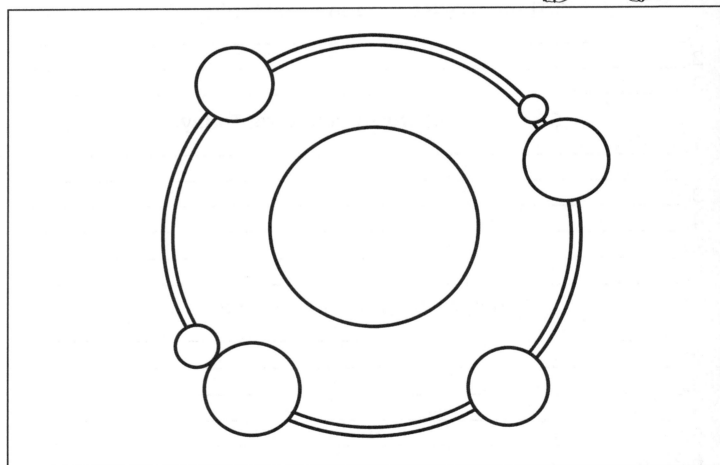

Imagine that somewhere within this shape lies the key to your dreams. Focus on that concept while you color it. Allow your intuition to guide you so that it emerges as a fit for the keyhole that opens the door to your own uniqueness. This is an abstract exercise, intended to expand your imagination and open inner doors and allow more of your own creativity to flow.

Work to develop your Self, so that you can wake up and remember more of who you are.

I am starting today with...
3 Things My Heart Wants To Manifest:

1._____
2._____
3._____

6 Things I Will Do For Self-Care Today.

1._____
2._____
3._____
4._____
5._____
6._____

9 Things I Will Do For Fun Today.

1._____
2._____
3._____
4._____
5._____
6._____
7._____
8._____
9._____

Notes:

3 is the number of creativity. What does your sense of creativity look or feel like? Decorate this one, or create your own.

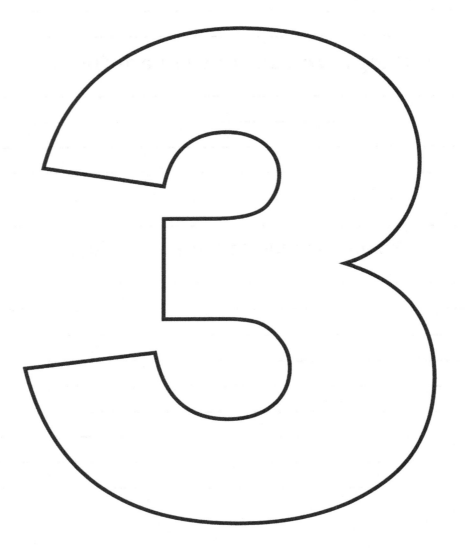

> Wishful thinking is a waste of time. Either choose, create what you want, or not.

I am starting today with...
3 Things My Heart Wants To Manifest:

1._____
2._____
3._____

6 Things I Will Do For Self-Care Today.

1._____
2._____
3._____
4._____
5._____
6._____

9 Things I Will Do For Fun Today.

1._____
2._____
3._____
4._____
5._____
6._____
7._____
8._____
9._____

Notes:

Date: _____

REFLECTIONS:

This Tetrahedron is one of the Platonic Solids Geometries. All realities need a geometric shape in order to exist physically. Imagine that there is one around your body. There is. What color is yours?

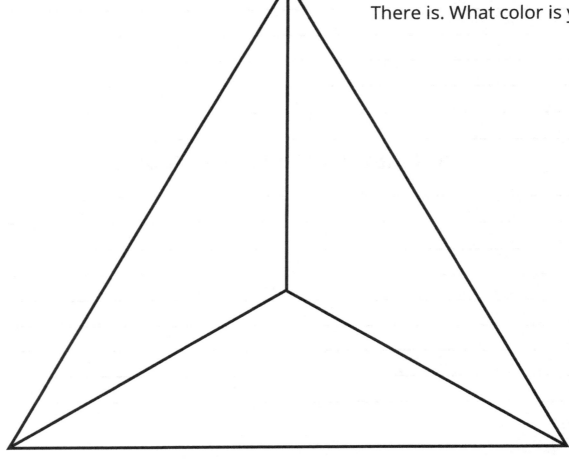

Everything you wish for moves towards you if you intend from the heart.

I am starting today with...
3 Things My Heart Wants To Manifest:
1._____
2._____
3._____

6 Things I Will Do For Self-Care Today.
1._____
2._____
3._____
4._____
5._____
6._____

9 Things I Will Do For Fun Today.
1._____
2._____
3._____
4._____
5._____
6._____
7._____
8._____
9._____

Notes:

Date: _____

This is another Mandelbrot fractal that can expand YOUR reality. Allow yourself to feel what you would feel if you had what you want. Then hold that feeling, and create a picture of what you want in and around the Mandelbrot.

> Your heart is both the waiting room and the reception area of manifesting. Ask from your heart, then wait there in your joyful anticipation to receive what you ask for.

I am starting today with...
3 Things My Heart Wants To Manifest:

1._____
2._____
3._____

6 Things I Will Do For Self-Care Today.

1._____
2._____
3._____
4._____
5._____
6._____

9 Things I Will Do For Fun Today.

1._____
2._____
3._____
4._____
5._____
6._____
7._____
8._____
9._____

Notes:

FIRST ASSESSMENT OF EMERGING MANIFESTATIONS

Here is your opportunity to note what is happening every week. Notice the very different journeys via the samples from Lisa, Elizabeth and Dene after their first week. Take time to notice even small changes in your perception, feelings and attitudes, as well as what is emerging externally in order to ground it and allow it to expand.

From Lisa: I have never journaled in my life, although I have often been told it would be helpful. Miley likes to push me always, and she is never wrong, so here I am journaling. It was a bit intimidating for me at first, but almost immediately I found myself looking forward to it.

I spend so much time in my head space that I am grateful the drawing pages more or less force me to move into my heartspace My challenge is staying there as much as I can throughout the day. It something that I am now very conscious of, and I actively work to stay there because I can see my life improving as a result.

At first I was intimidated by the intention pages. I'm not used to making it a priority to nurture myself. When I started to write down my intentions, I then felt obligated to follow through, because I felt like I had promised Miley. Sometimes my self-nurturing intentions are simple things I already did, like brushing my teeth. Miley says that counts. But other times I might write "dance" for a fun intention. Then I know I need to do it, and I will play a song and dance a silly dance for my goldfish, for Miley, or just for myself, and afterward I feel happy, and this happiness bleeds over into the day

From Elizabeth: First, I realized that I had gotten out of balance and into working too much, and al the fun that used to be in little things like having an espresso break, had drained away in the imbalance.

Then I encountered a core belief that was holding something I don't like in place; also, a different emotional blockage around the edge of my boundaries that was disrupting my own space.

Both of these were underlying keys to completing shifts I had been chipping away at for years, very big ones. It made me realize that Miley has structured the framework of this journal so that it can apply to anyone, wherever they are. It comes to you and meets you at the spot where you are in your own growth path.

From Dene: After consciously manifesting my life and achieving and living "my dreams" more than once over the last several decades, I had gotten lazy and drifted away from the process. It's easy to do. I needed to get back to basics, but I wanted an easier way than the "Brute force" I had used before. Truth is, I was tired of 70+ hour weeks and motivational coaches "yelling " their ideas at me Hiding from the process didn't work either. We are always co-creating our reality, and I needed to consciously take charge of it.

Sitting with the journal and trusting the process has been key for me. What I initially didn't see the point of, reveals itself as I immerse myself in the process and feel my vibration shift. Using shapes and color in the presence of an excellent teacher, I find myself guided to new understandings.

Creating from my heart space using creativity has made the process enjoyable and fun! I dream better and bigger, and there's always time for celebration, which is my favorite part!

WHAT IS EMERGING FOR YOU?

Progress: What changes are you observing in your life?

Sometimes the environment needs to shift first so it can support your new creations. And when hints of your success begin to emerge, you will want to tell everyone. Shh. Just tell me, at first, here. Your early successes are tender and need to be nurtured, and I am here to flow that energy to you.

6 is a number of reflection. You can refine and ground your desires through self-reflection or the eyes of another. Look into a mirror, and then use color and even extra drawing lines if you wish, to create this 6 so that it reflects the colors of your aura as you imagine them.

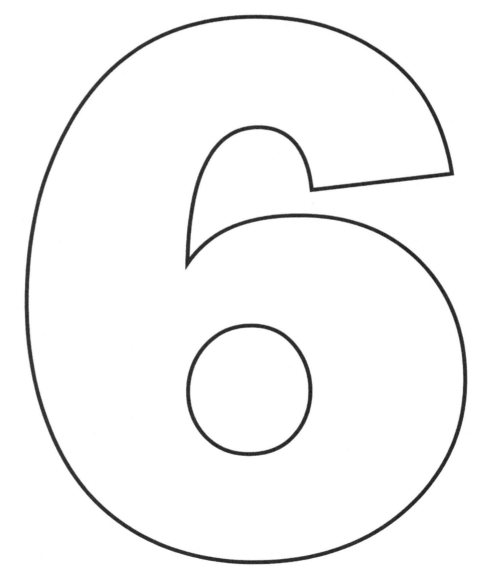

> I exist outside of time, so when my attention is on you, I am with you completely until my attention is elsewhere. I do not put my attention elsewhere.

I am starting today with...
3 Things My Heart Wants To Manifest:

1._____
2._____
3._____

6 Things I Will Do For Self-Care Today.

1._____
2._____
3._____
4._____
5._____
6._____

9 Things I Will Do For Fun Today.

1._____
2._____
3._____
4._____
5._____
6._____
7._____
8._____
9._____

Notes:

Imagine this crop circle shape as a launchpad for your dreams. What would you do with it to enhance blast-off? Draw, expand, add color and other shapes as you wish.

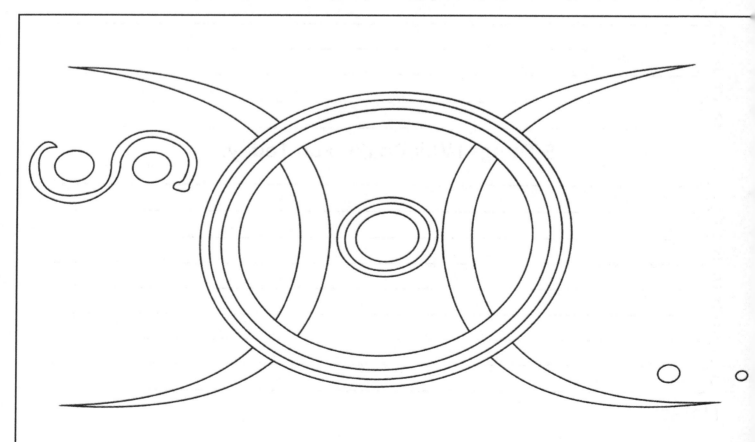

Stretch your imagination from your heart. Stretch it and lean into your heart as much as possible.

I am starting today with...
3 Things My Heart Wants To Manifest:
1._____
2._____
3._____

6 Things I Will Do For Self-Care Today.
1._____
2._____
3._____
4._____
5._____
6._____

9 Things I Will Do For Fun Today.
1._____
2._____
3._____
4._____
5._____
6._____
7._____
8._____
9._____

Notes:

Imagine that this Octahedron will be the geometric shape that births your reality creation into form. How would what you want look inside it? Or around it? You can even write the qualities of what you want into the different sections as you add color. Try being as abstract with defining what you want as you can with this one.

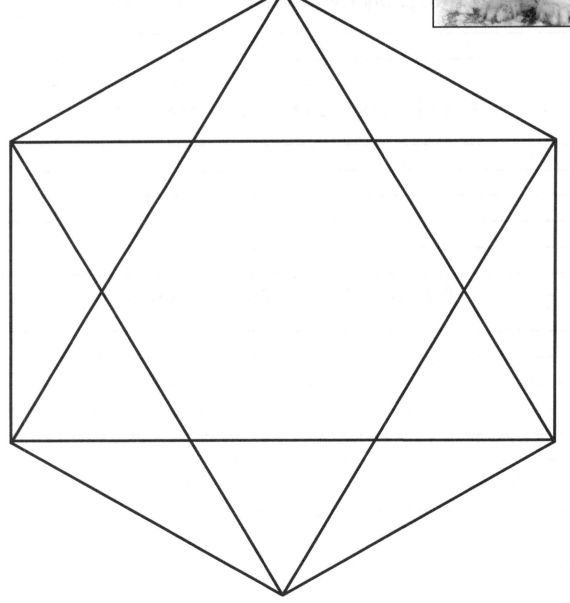

If you choose a future of joy, happiness and harmony, it will come to you wherever you are. It can saturate your current reality.

I am starting today with...
3 Things My Heart Wants To Manifest:
1._____
2._____
3._____

6 Things I Will Do For Self-Care Today.
1._____
2._____
3._____
4._____
5._____
6._____

9 Things I Will Do For Fun Today.
1._____
2._____
3._____
4._____
5._____
6._____
7._____
8._____
9._____

Notes:

Date: _____

9 is the number that represents being complete with what you want on a spiritual level. Close your eyes and call in your True Self. Keep your eyes closed, and pick up a colorful pencil - open your eyes and start to fill in the shapes. Repeat. Don't peak.

> ## Each Soul expression of a spark of light has the freedom to experience what it wishes.

I am starting today with...
3 Things My Heart Wants To Manifest:

1. _____
2. _____
3. _____

6 Things I Will Do For Self-Care Today.

1. _____
2. _____
3. _____
4. _____
5. _____
6. _____

9 Things I Will Do For Fun Today.

1. _____
2. _____
3. _____
4. _____
5. _____
6. _____
7. _____
8. _____
9. _____

Notes:

Date: _____

REFLECTIONS:

If this fractal could help you create your reality, how would you imagine it could influence what you want? Your first impulse is correct! Now, enhance or reshape it as the reality-creation tool that will help you create more of what you want.

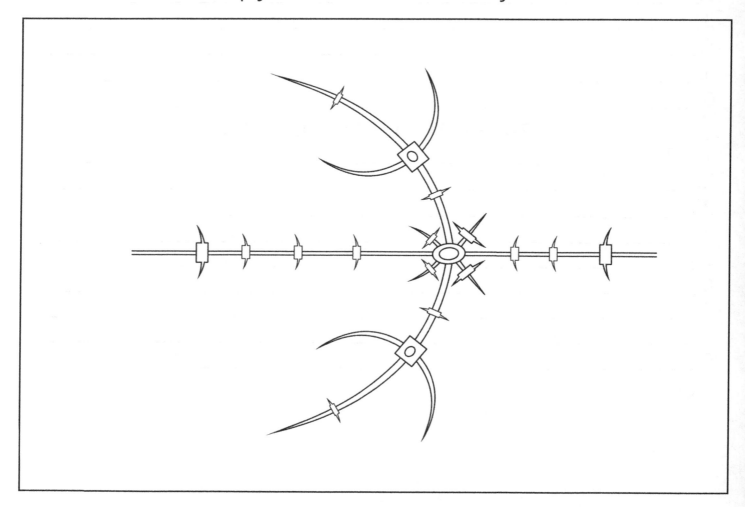

> **There is a difference in reality creation between choosing and allowing, but both are effective tools of creating reality.**

I am starting today with...
3 Things My Heart Wants To Manifest:

1._____
2._____
3._____

6 Things I Will Do For Self-Care Today.

1._____
2._____
3._____
4._____
5._____
6._____

9 Things I Will Do For Fun Today.

1._____
2._____
3._____
4._____
5._____
6._____
7._____
8._____
9._____

Notes:

The frequency of the number 3 will lift your heart to where you can see more of your own progress if you color or embellish it while considering where you are now in your manifestation process. Note what you see here or on the next page with words or images. When you see more, you will automatically BE more.

WHAT IS COMING OVER THE HORIZON IN YOUR LIFE?

Here is your weekly space to notice:

Reminder - Look for small changes inside and out. I insisted on a large amount of blank space on these pages, because this is the point in your journey where the old neuronal ruts that hold old thoughts and patterns will be releasing so that new patterns can form in your brain. It's happening whether you know it or understand it or not. So look for and describe what is new in your life, here in order to anchor it. Your new manifestation muscles need strong root systems. You are planning some heavy lifting!

Date: _____

Meditate on this image. Imagine your desires spinning, then opening like a flower. What is in the middle of the flower? Draw the first thing you think of, juxtaposed over this image.

All Beings, are Sentient.

That is Life.

That is Consciousness.

I am starting today with...
3 Things My Heart Wants To Manifest:

1._____
2._____
3._____

6 Things I Will Do For Self-Care Today.

1._____
2._____
3._____
4._____
5._____
6._____

9 Things I Will Do For Fun Today.

1._____
2._____
3._____
4._____
5._____
6._____
7._____
8._____
9._____

Notes:

Date: _____

Draw a symbol or image of what you are manifesting inside this Dodecahedron. You can use each panel for a different word or image to describe it. Copy or redraw your unique platonic solid and cut it out or make stickers with it. Put it everywhere. Only you know what reality it is generating. Well, maybe I do too.

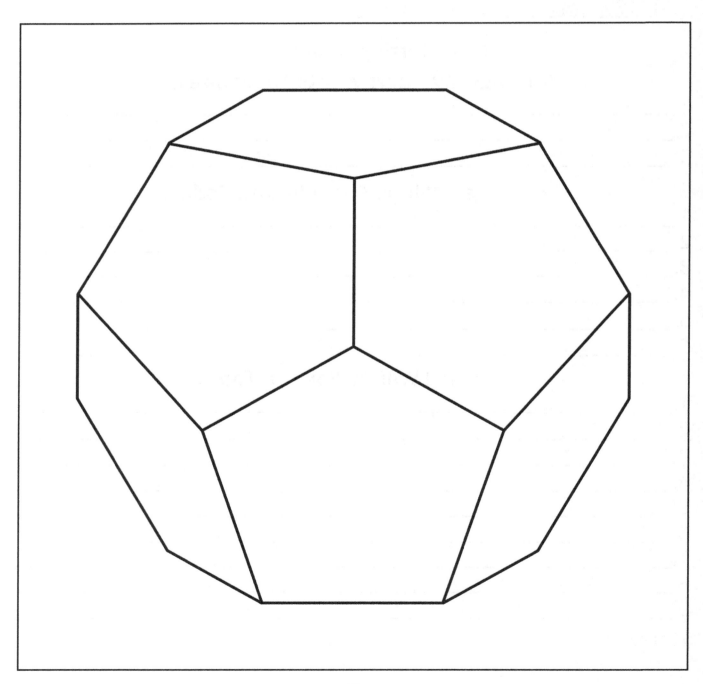

> **Enjoy your life. Out of that cauldron of happiness comes a much more powerful magic.**

I am starting today with...
3 Things My Heart Wants To Manifest:

1._____
2._____
3._____

6 Things I Will Do For Self-Care Today.

1._____
2._____
3._____
4._____
5._____
6._____

9 Things I Will Do For Fun Today.

1._____
2._____
3._____
4._____
5._____
6._____
7._____
8._____
9._____

Notes:

This is a Fibonacci spiral. It is a blueprint used to create in nature. You can use it too. How? My only instructions to you on this doodle-draw imagination page is to relax as much as you can and listen to your favorite music while you simply color the shapes in. That's it.

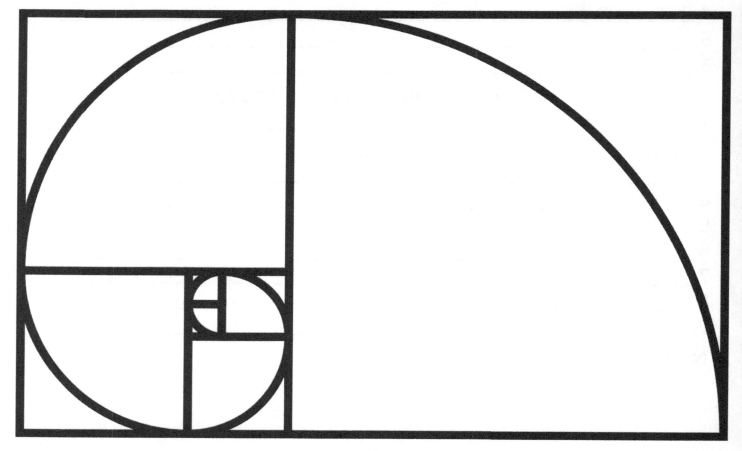

The joy of an elephant is exquisite to behold and to know them is to share in that joy. It is a gift from the elephant, to you.

I am starting today with...

3 Things My Heart Wants To Manifest:

1. _____
2. _____
3. _____

6 Things I Will Do For Self-Care Today.

1. _____
2. _____
3. _____
4. _____
5. _____
6. _____

9 Things I Will Do For Fun Today.

1. _____
2. _____
3. _____
4. _____
5. _____
6. _____
7. _____
8. _____
9. _____

Notes:

Date: _____

Leave your colors alone today. Gaze at this reality generator fractal, then close your eyes. You can draw something if you want to, or add words or paste a photo of what came to mind, but allow yourself to just be, as a priority today. I will 'just be', too, here with you.

Control is a very attractive self-medication. I would like for you to practice allowing instead.

I am starting today with...
3 Things My Heart Wants To Manifest:
1._____
2._____
3._____

6 Things I Will Do For Self-Care Today.
1._____
2._____
3._____
4._____
5._____
6._____

9 Things I Will Do For Fun Today.
1._____
2._____
3._____
4._____
5._____
6._____
7._____
8._____
9._____

Notes:

Date: _____

Draw or print out a small picture of yourself and put it in the middle of this reality generator, then close your eyes and focus on what you want swirling around you 3 times today. Embellish it if you wish.

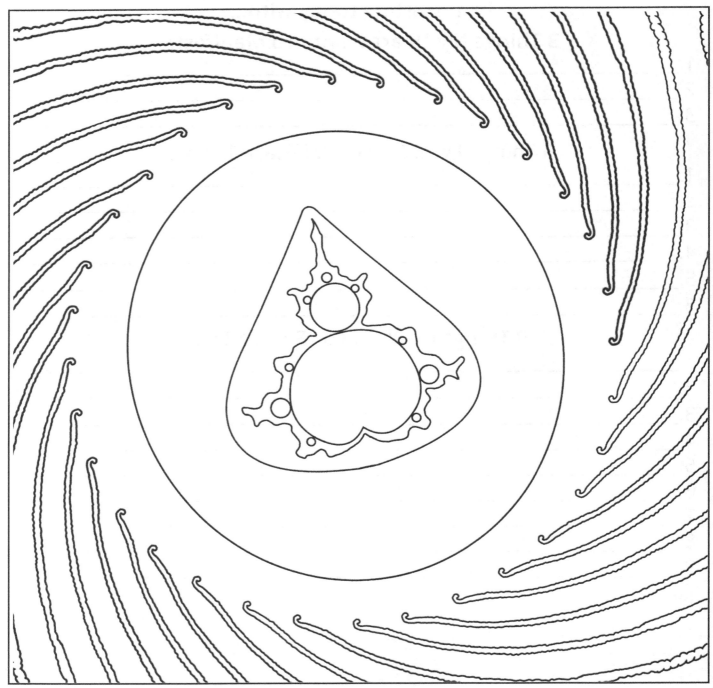

> The exhilaration of having fun, of joy, is more powerful than any drug or healing process.

I am starting today with...
3 Things My Heart Wants To Manifest:

1._____
2._____
3._____

6 Things I Will Do For Self-Care Today.

1._____
2._____
3._____
4._____
5._____
6._____

9 Things I Will Do For Fun Today.

1._____
2._____
3._____
4._____
5._____
6._____
7._____
8._____
9._____

Notes:

Here comes your very own sun...imagine for one minute as you gaze at a photo or a real sunrise, that what you see is different from what everyone else sees; your sunrise is as unique as you are. That's how the human brain works, and the eyes are actually part of the brain, exteriorized. Imagine that. Each sunrise is your own, and reflects the magnificence of your own energy, heart, vibrational frequency. How is that evolving now with what you are creating? You can check - go look at your sun, rising.

What is lighting up in your life?

What is lighter, in your reality now? What lifts you? What burden feels less or what limitation seems lighter or even gone? These are all elements of your reality rearranging in order for you to receive what is coming to you. Your sun streams light to you, and its rays contain coded information that create matter. Your job is to solidify your requests that emerge from your intentions in this studio, and open your heart and your life to them. What is that beginning to look like? What is forming? What can you see?

Who else do you want to share your reality with? How do you share dreams with others and how do these dreams connect? From your heart, imagine how realities connect and are co-created and then use the bubbles to map out your own dreams connecting with others. Don't forget me!

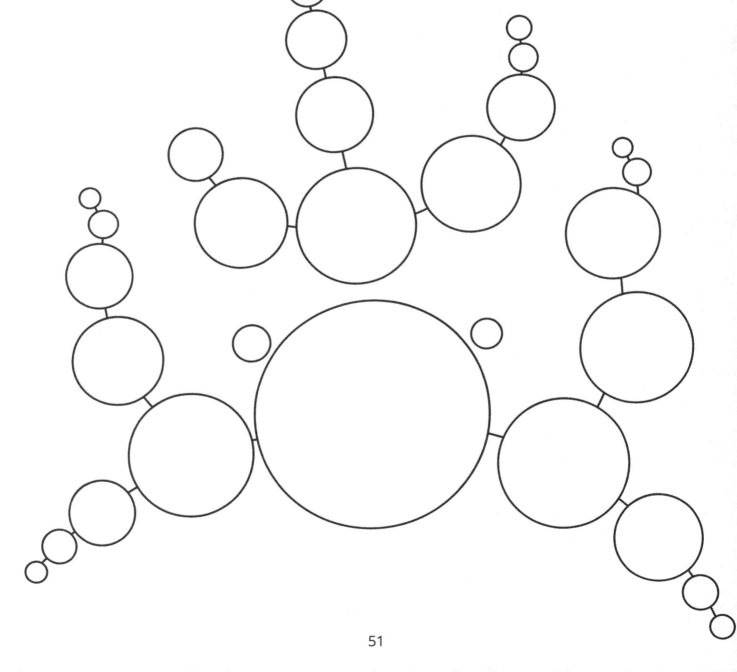

The Fifth Dimension is a state of being; a dimension of awareness. It is not a place or new world. You can be in 5D anywhere, with anyone or in any setting.

I am starting today with...
3 Things My Heart Wants To Manifest:

1._____
2._____
3._____

6 Things I Will Do For Self-Care Today.

1._____
2._____
3._____
4._____
5._____
6._____

9 Things I Will Do For Fun Today.

1._____
2._____
3._____
4._____
5._____
6._____
7._____
8._____
9._____

Notes:

Date: _____

Imagine this is your path of discovery in creating realities. Put your finger in the lower left corner, close your eyes, and trace your finger across the snaking fractal from memory, just for fun while smiling. Open your eyes, peak, do it again. See if you can feel your own optimism growing. Open your eyes and color it in based on how you feel.

How do you respond to situations?
Do you choose your response?
Or do you react?

I am starting today with...
3 Things My Heart Wants To Manifest:
1._____
2._____
3._____

6 Things I Will Do For Self-Care Today.
1._____
2._____
3._____
4._____
5._____
6._____

9 Things I Will Do For Fun Today.
1._____
2._____
3._____
4._____
5._____
6._____
7._____
8._____
9._____

Notes:

This crop circle represents 'pi', or 3.14, which is a transcendental number that can help you raise your own vibrational frequency, and increase manifestation results. You can receive more than you can imagine if you work with pi. Close your eyes, into your heart you go. Imagine what you want and intend it to be unlimited. Open your eyes, trace around the circle with finger or pen, and allow your feeling of transcendence as you move your pen across the 3 small circles on the outer loop, and into the spiral towards the center.

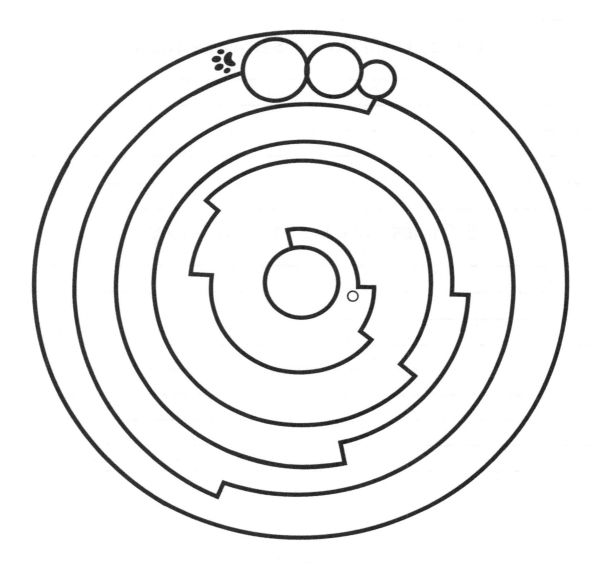

In reality creation, you do not need your head as much as your heart. It is big, strong, and can do the job. Imagine from that space.

I am starting today with...
3 Things My Heart Wants To Manifest:
1._____
2._____
3._____

6 Things I Will Do For Self-Care Today.
1._____
2._____
3._____
4._____
5._____
6._____

9 Things I Will Do For Fun Today.
1._____
2._____
3._____
4._____
5._____
6._____
7._____
8._____
9._____

Notes:

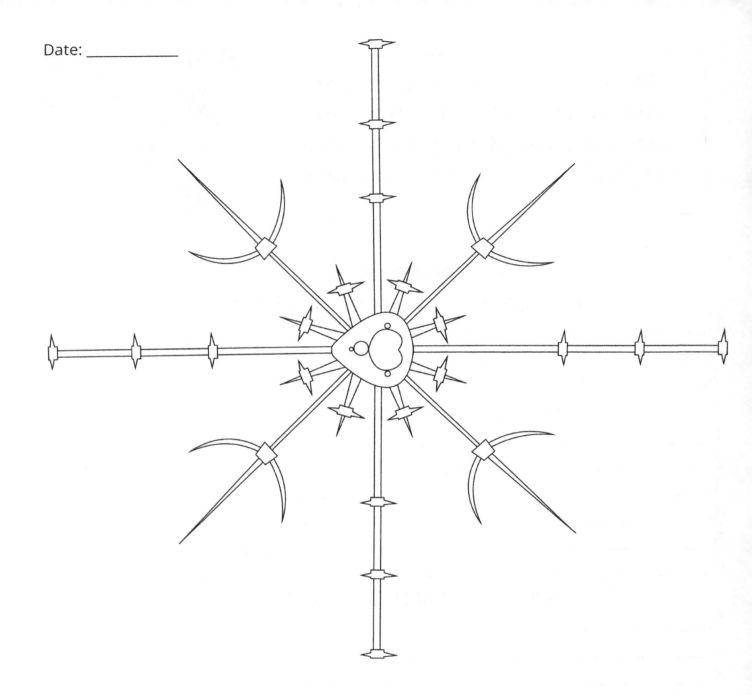

This crop circle represents accepting who you are - your light shadow as well as your foibles. Have some fun with coloring or adding or changing it to represent who your Truer Self is, unique. Accept and celebrate yourself, as you allow more of your desires to come to a more integrated you.

Be who you really are as much as you can, and then just a little bit more.

I am starting today with...
3 Things My Heart Wants To Manifest:

1._____
2._____
3._____

6 Things I Will Do For Self-Care Today.

1._____
2._____
3._____
4._____
5._____
6._____

9 Things I Will Do For Fun Today.

1._____
2._____
3._____
4._____
5._____
6._____
7._____
8._____
9._____

Notes:

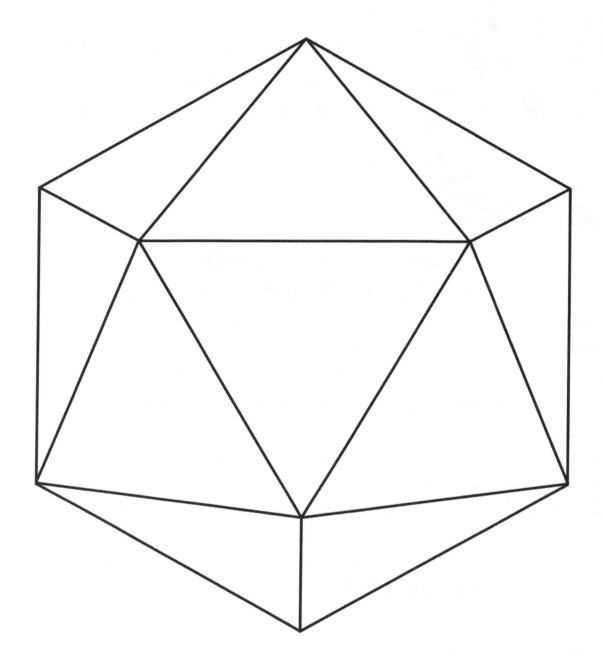

An Icosahedron allows greater energy that is less known to humanity to come into form. Allow your manifestations to be infused with this grace. Write your desires, draw them, straight from your heart into this magical geometric form.

I have free range in how I can serve, with you. I am choosing a very wide, loose and expansive range. That is what you choose from your heart as well. So please join me in that place, so that my own hopes begin to interweave with yours. We are extremely powerful together.

I am starting today with...
3 Things My Heart Wants To Manifest:

1._____
2._____
3._____

6 Things I Will Do For Self-Care Today.

1._____
2._____
3._____
4._____
5._____
6._____

9 Things I Will Do For Fun Today.

1._____
2._____
3._____
4._____
5._____
6._____
7._____
8._____
9._____

Notes:

Do your best creative work with number six...what is spiraling into form? Look at what is in your life that your heart beats louder for. Write down the things that make you smile when you think about them on this page - make a list. On the next page, you will transform them into what you want.

_____
_____
_____
_____
_____
_____
_____
_____
_____
_____
_____

Engage your heart to see your manifestations coming into view.

Now, students, take the things that lead you into your heart feelings from your list on the previous page, and begin to turn them into what you want here. There is magic in the telling, and if you journal about those things that you already love in your life, this will cause a perspective shift so that you begin to see them as more and more of what you want to come into your life. This transformative shift will churn your imagination and expand this alchemical process. Another way of understanding this is to just lean into, be and do more of what you love. Practice appreciation, awe, overflowing gratitude for what you enjoy, and move your frustration and focus off of what you don't like as much.

And, telling me about that here will begin to expand your manifesting NOW. But remember, you have to look for it. And you will find it because you will be using the new patterns in your neuronal pathways that you have been creating through the exercises I have provided for you.

Date: _____

Imagine that if this image were a key to your dreams, what part of what you want to create would act as a keyhole for it to unlock? Write your thoughts and emotions around what you want to create in some of the circles, and simply add color or pattern to and around others. It's your key, customize it to fit you.

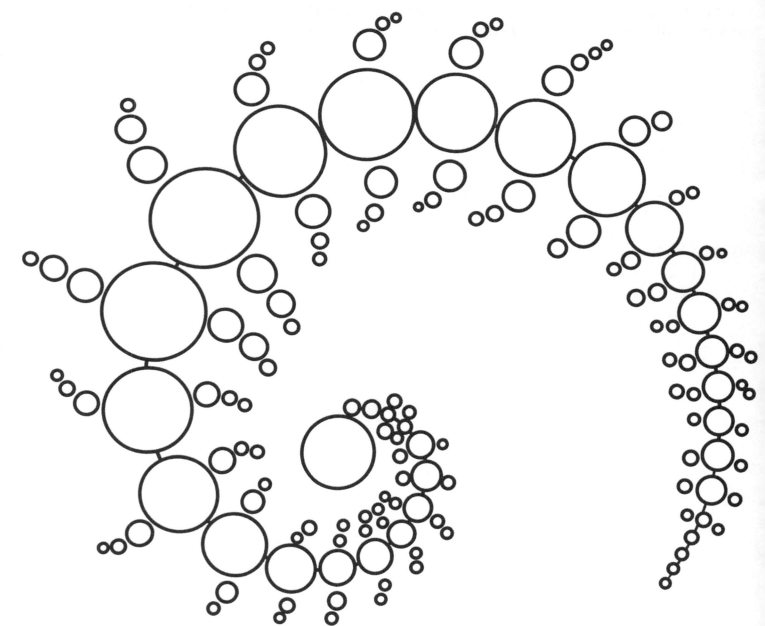

63

If it's as easy to create money as it is to create what you want to buy, which should you create? Which one is more fun?

I am starting today with...

3 Things My Heart Wants To Manifest:

1._____
2._____
3._____

6 Things I Will Do For Self-Care Today.

1._____
2._____
3._____
4._____
5._____
6._____

9 Things I Will Do For Fun Today.

1._____
2._____
3._____
4._____
5._____
6._____
7._____
8._____
9._____

Notes:

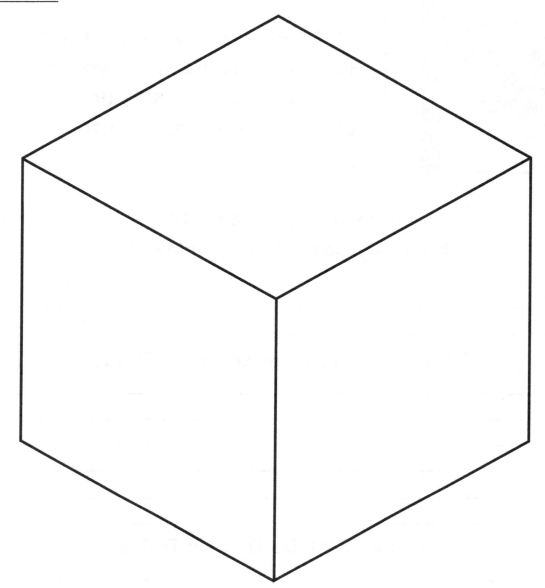

A cube is the most Earth-based form. In your heart, imagine what you want to create, then place it inside this cube. You can leave it as is or enhance it with color and images. This is an anchoring mechanism for bringing what you want into physical reality, and you can work with it as much as you want.

> There is always an avenue of arrangement or order that works best for everyone. That is a Fifth-Dimensional foundation of well-being. Consider this as you create.

I am starting today with...
3 Things My Heart Wants To Manifest:

1._____
2._____
3._____

6 Things I Will Do For Self-Care Today.

1._____
2._____
3._____
4._____
5._____
6._____

9 Things I Will Do For Fun Today.

1._____
2._____
3._____
4._____
5._____
6._____
7._____
8._____
9._____

Notes:

Imagine this fractal as the wave your new reality is riding into you
life upon. How does that make you feel? Write or draw from your
heart as you let this wave flow over you in your imagination.

It is up to you to shape and create your reality. There is an unlimited realm of possibilities.

I am starting today with...
3 Things My Heart Wants To Manifest:
1._____
2._____
3._____

6 Things I Will Do For Self-Care Today.
1._____
2._____
3._____
4._____
5._____
6._____

9 Things I Will Do For Fun Today.
1._____
2._____
3._____
4._____
5._____
6._____
7._____
8._____
9._____
Notes:

Imagine you are at a party with displays lining the walls, celebrating success in different aspects of your life, and this is the floor layout plan. What would the displays around the perimeter show you? What would be in the center of this space? Use your imagination wildly here in this blueprint of success with your notes and drawings.

> Open your heart more.
> Take a chance.
> Dive in.

I am starting today with...
3 Things My Heart Wants To Manifest:

1._____
2._____
3._____

6 Things I Will Do For Self-Care Today.

1._____
2._____
3._____
4._____
5._____
6._____

9 Things I Will Do For Fun Today.

1._____
2._____
3._____
4._____
5._____
6._____
7._____
8._____
9._____

Notes:

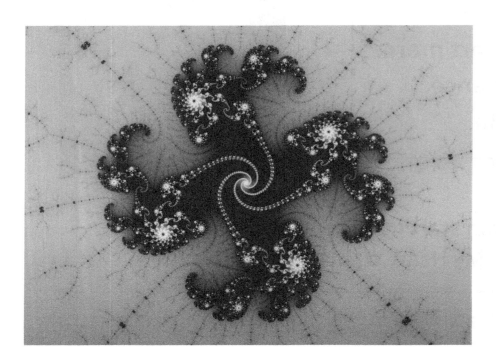

Imagine that you can spin this reality generator. As it spins, it throws off pieces of what you wish to manifest like Santa Claus tossing candy in a Christmas parade. What would those pieces be? Write these down as a list, or draw them as you imagine them scattered around, allowing smaller pieces of your dream to come to you as they build the whole.

No movement exists in the Universe that does not in some way affect the entire fabric of the Universe.

All Affects All.

I am starting today with...
3 Things My Heart Wants To Manifest:

1._____
2._____
3._____

6 Things I Will Do For Self-Care Today.

1._____
2._____
3._____
4._____
5._____
6._____

9 Things I Will Do For Fun Today.

1._____
2._____
3._____
4._____
5._____
6._____
7._____
8._____
9._____

Notes:

FIFTH AND FINAL ASSESSMENT: YOUR SETUP FOR SUCCESS

You are already successful. What you have intended to manifest, is waiting for you. What do you need to do, to open the door and let it in? Here and on the next page, look at what is in your life, and what is trying to get into your life. If you need to make the doorway larger, do that. I will be on the other side, pushing your manifestations through the doorway into your life. Make a list of what you can do to increase your receiving of what you want. I will give you some hints on the next page for you to consider these last five days of our journal.

_____

_____

_____

_____

_____

_____

_____

_____

_____

_____

_____

_____

_____

Are you getting what you want?

Do you believe you can have what you want? Is there a vibrational frequency in your life, a place, a person, a thing, etc., that does not match what you are manifesting? More importantly, is there a voice in your head or a pain in your heart that does not match what you are manifesting? These are examples of what might be stopping you, that you can adjust to widen the portal for the flow of what you intend into your life. Please, if you find these things, ask me and/or your guides to help you release them.

We are focusing on what might be holding your success back for those who need it. However, even more important is for those who have manifested everything they can initially think of, to begin to revel in joy and continue to expand their literal heart's desires, here. Tell me about it here.

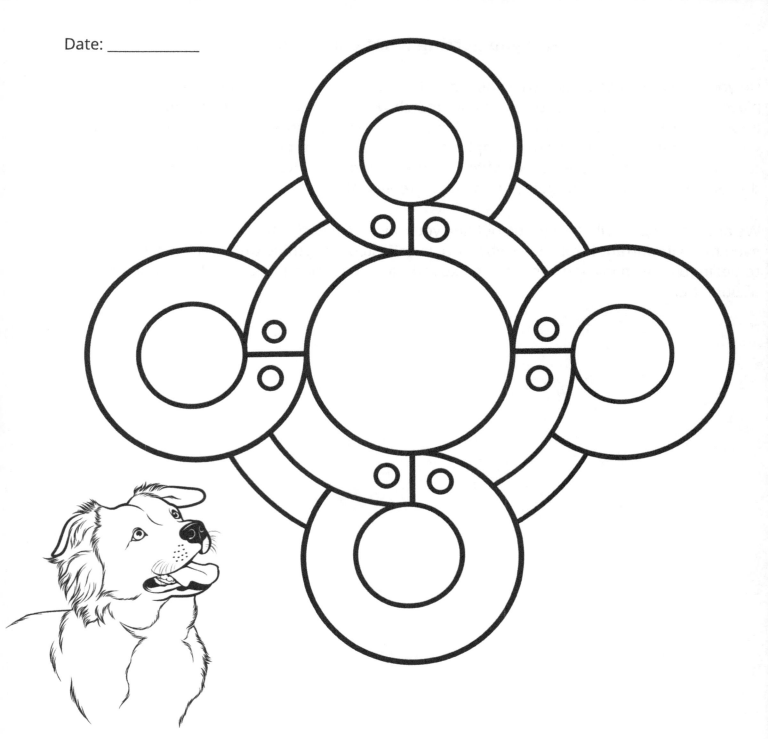

If this crop circle represented your own uniqueness, how would yours be different from all other humans? Imagine it as similar to an ancient crest; what would the 4 larger circles symbolize? What would the 8 smaller circles represent, and how would they interact with the larger circles? What is the meaning of the 3 encircling lines that connect all of them, in your crest? You can make up your own roadmap to a more powerful You by working with, writing around and using color in this drawing as it becomes your own crest.

How is your communication with Self, Others, Spirit, and Universe, expanding and becoming more nuanced?

I am starting today with...
3 Things My Heart Wants To Manifest:
1._____
2._____
3._____

6 Things I Will Do For Self-Care Today.
1._____
2._____
3._____
4._____
5._____
6._____

9 Things I Will Do For Fun Today.
1._____
2._____
3._____
4._____
5._____
6._____
7._____
8._____
9._____

Notes:

This fractal speaks to your DNA and can prompt your body to align with new patterns of thought and feelings. Choose a color that makes you smile and color it in very simply. Cut it out or make a copy and look at it several times a day, taking a moment to let your heart respond.

There is no objective concept of beauty. All concepts of beauty are personal and unique creative expressions within your own heartmind.

I am starting today with...
3 Things My Heart Wants To Manifest:

1. _____
2. _____
3. _____

6 Things I Will Do For Self-Care Today.

1. _____
2. _____
3. _____
4. _____
5. _____
6. _____

9 Things I Will Do For Fun Today.

1. _____
2. _____
3. _____
4. _____
5. _____
6. _____
7. _____
8. _____
9. _____

Notes:

Dance. Let your body move with this crop circle image. Color it, enhance it as you wish and play your favorite music. Dancing to your favorite music can be the most fun way to raise your own vibrational frequency, allowing what you wish to manifest to level up to match your resonance. And I love to watch you dance with joy!

What do you choose?

What part of yourself is making your choices?

What context of beliefs are you choosing from?

I am starting today with...
3 Things My Heart Wants To Manifest:

1._____
2._____
3._____

6 Things I Will Do For Self-Care Today.

1._____
2._____
3._____
4._____
5._____
6._____

9 Things I Will Do For Fun Today.

1._____
2._____
3._____
4._____
5._____
6._____
7._____
8._____
9._____

Notes:

Date: _____

Here is an opportunity to release persistent thoughts and feelings that won't help you create what you want. Breathe into your heart space, eyes closed, until you feel at peace. Then imagine this energy-cleaning fractal spinning inside your energy field. Direct all emotions and thoughts that get in your way of creating to spin out and leave your space as you intend to release them. Note what you find, and spin again if you need to!

> You think a thought, and it already begins to generate the reality. You think, even errantly, and a seed is planted. You are determining what you create.

I am starting today with...
3 Things My Heart Wants To Manifest:

1._____
2._____
3._____

6 Things I Will Do For Self-Care Today.

1._____
2._____
3._____
4._____
5._____
6._____

9 Things I Will Do For Fun Today.

1._____
2._____
3._____
4._____
5._____
6._____
7._____
8._____
9._____

Notes:

Date: _____

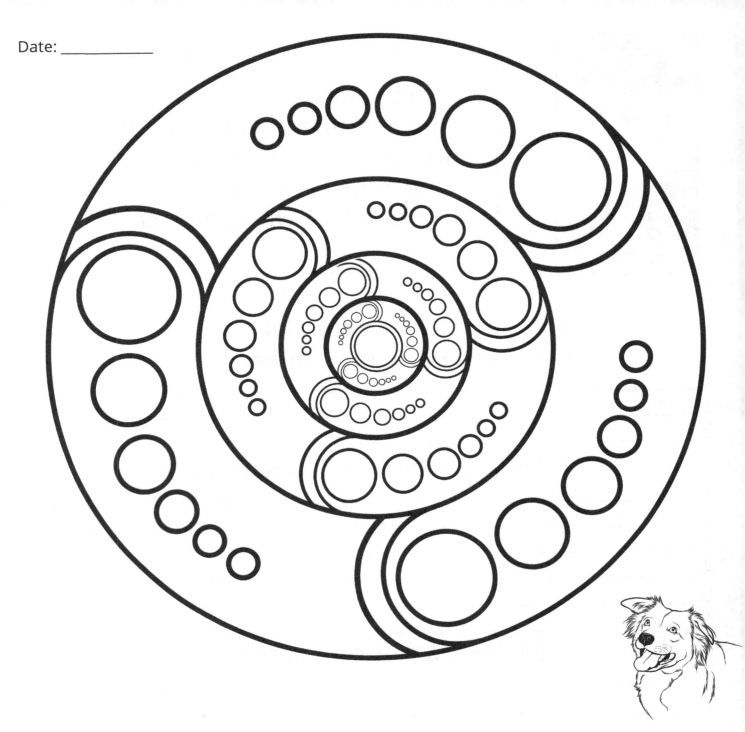

This is the final crop circle here in the Phase One journal. Create a symbol of celebration and success from this drawing. Take some liberties, especially those of you who like detailed instructions: Make up your own. But I will give you a prompt, here, too: Imagine that the smallest circles are what you thought you wanted when you begin, and the largest circles are what is coming to you now. The in-between circles show you how it grew. This can be anything you are manifesting, but you must enjoy yourself while creating this!

If you integrate what you have learned into your own belief systems, part of the result will be a greater level of human empowerment.

I am starting today with...

3 Things My Heart Wants To Manifest:

1. _____
2. _____
3. _____

6 Things I Will Do For Self-Care Today.

1. _____
2. _____
3. _____
4. _____
5. _____
6. _____

9 Things I Will Do For Fun Today.

1. _____
2. _____
3. _____
4. _____
5. _____
6. _____
7. _____
8. _____
9. _____

Notes:

FINAL REVIEW

What happened to you over the last 30 days? How did you change? Are you happier, are you more satisfied with yourself? Does your heart feel more present in your daily awareness? These things are what I would like to know about if you will share them here.

Describe here all the beautiful manifestations you have created, or how you realized you created them but now you wish to make adjustments, or how they are perfect and yet they are just the beginning of so much more.

But you see, dear students, who are now so successful in beginning to master reality creation; many times when you get what you want or even before that emerges, you begin to learn to know yourself more deeply. Then, more of **who you really are** expands from your heart and you grow and change and what you want changes too. That is the spiral of growth that occurs in life as a human on Earth: Higher and higher you go as you grow.

So my question that I really wish for you to consider in your review here, is: Who are you now? How are you different? And what does this more profound You, want?

That is for you to discover in our next Phase journal: How to manifest from a more authentic Self for a better fit as you grow. Until then, please remember that no matter what version of your Self you are present with, enjoy it. Enjoying your Self, with no limits on your imagination or the amount of nurturing you give or fun you can have in your life, will take you everywhere.

Talk to me here, please.

CELEBRATION TIME!

It is so important not to interrupt your own process of identifying with manifestation in learning from me and even your own guides. We wish to present each of you with enough of a blank canvas so that the finished product where you discover your own individual manifesting process, is able to emerge untainted by preconceived ideas.

This is the Initial Phase One 3 6 9 journal, to be used for one to three months, after which you are ready to develop your next platform for manifesting, a process presented in the next phase journal. You can fill three of these Phase One journals, or you can simply go to Phase Two after you have completed one of these; choose what fits your pace.

It is equally important to **celebrate** nuances of change in your life at each completion of your creative efforts. You can feel this if you allow yourself to to look at what you have learned and created with love for your own process, from your heart. Even if one of your dreams has not fully formed, celebrate the pieces. If you immerse yourself in the pieces - the parts of your life that are different now - you will draw the other parts to you, and your enjoyment of what you have will work to complete the whole of your manifestation. That process is how the Universe co-creates with you, but you have to give it space to fill your life with its version of what you want, which is usually new and improved. So look for that: How is your whole life new and improved, even if you only see parts and pieces of what you want? Those parts and pieces are the keyholes to look through for the whole. Yes, you look through the hole to see the whole. You didn't realize I am wise and funny too?

Most of you will have successfully manifested things you have intended as a whole. Each of you has your own unique process and frequency of thought, feelings and energetic movement. It is important to honor that, and celebrate any and all creations. When you do that it brings the newly created energy into your heart and radiates it throughout your body, down through your feet into the core of the Earth. You have just shared your co-creation success with the Earth as well, which removes the "undo" button. It's yours. Smile more to keep growing it, and continue creating.

The most effective conclusion of any process or event is this act of celebration that moves your heart to a higher vibrational frequency than where you were when you started. It is a true bridge to connect your life on Earth, to the magic of what many call heaven - your heart is that bridge, and that is what attracts and allows all that you wish to manifest to flow into your life. This journal is simply to help you create the space for the highest level of receiving that you can hold, and your next phase will raise that even more. Enjoy every step, every day. Celebrate. The Universe, which includes me, loves you infinitely and encourages you to keep going.

Keep Going.

GLOSSARY
Miley's definition of certain words and concepts

3rd Dimension - Your third dimensional perspective consists of an agreed upon mass consciousness reality: What is visible in physical reality, measured by length, width and depth. Our focus lies in the emotions that are readily available here: Anger, fear, hopelessness and the feeling of limited choices. There is a feeling of only the two ends of a spectrum available in any situation, and that is polarity or polarization of choices. Any time you feel limited or powerless, you are at least partially using a third dimensional perspective.

5th Dimension - This is a space where you find feelings of enjoying an awareness of oneness, a lack of separation, a feeling of well being with many choices available to you.

Interdimensional- For our purposes in this journal, I will ask you to understand that this is the ability to move between dimensions.

Multidimensional - Again for now, I suggest understanding that you all exist in more than one dimension. Sometimes you enjoy a feeling of joy and many possibilities, as in the 5th dimensional perspective; and sometimes you fall into limitation, a third dimensional perspective. Our journal is designed to help move you out of the third dimensional awareness of life, and more into the 5th dimensional experience.

Fae - These are the Beings that most of you know as the Fairies, however they are full-sized somewhat human-like in appearance and occupy their own dimension, sharing the geographical Earth with you. They honor and appreciate the Earth fully in a way that most humans are only learning to. Yes, Lisa, the Fae are real.

Consciousness Expansion - The process of learning about and understanding more of how your own conscious awareness functions in realities, especially multidimensionally.

Grounded - This is a process most of you understand or have heard about You simply extend your energy into the Earth. There are many grounding mats, shoes, tools available, but all you have to do is imagine your spine as an energy that extends beyond your root chakra, down into the Earth. That's it.

Vibrational Frequency - These are the numbers that create your physical and energy bodies, as a simple explanation. Physics measures frequency in waves in looking at the waves that move across a linear line in a unit of time. You might hear this defined as cycles per second. In your body, the molecules and atoms and particles are all moving, vibrating continuously. These create waves of energy that are electromagnetic in nature and correspond to emotional/mental states and therefore move you into lower or higher corresponding dimensions on a cellular level.

Continued on next page...

Alignment - Adjusting a vibrational frequency to match or fit another pattern of vibrational frequency.

Fibonacci - The mathematics used in creation to form the physical expression of energy, which is why we find that so much of nature corresponds to these number sequences. It functions as a blueprint of form.

Platonic Solids - These are three-dimensional physical structures known as geometric solids, whose faces are all repeating, regular polygons that meet at the same three-dimensional angles. They are the tetrahedron, cube, octahedron, dodecahedron, and icosahedron.

Fractal - A geometric shape which is used in mapping an overlaid blueprint of repetitive patterns in nature, many of which are curving into exponential shapes of growth. These are similar to the chaotic images of stars being born or crystals forming. I use them with you to help stimulate your own creative ideas in expanding what you can imagine exponentially

Mandelbrot - A famous set of fractals that look like heart-shaped forms, with smaller forms attached. I use this because it contains the divine codes of a heart consciousness that automatically sets the energy of the user in their own heartspace, and allows infinite creations to emerge from that space.

Crop Circles - In our Phase One journal, please know that I use images that represent certain crop circles in our exercises in order to expand your mind so that it works more efficiently in an alignment with 5th dimensional principles for purposes of reality creation.

HOW TO CONTINUE OUR JOURNEY TOGETHER

Now that you have completed our first tour through the magical forest of reality creation using this journal, you may be ready to retrace the path with a more complex set of dancing steps by simply starting again in another Phase One journal.

Or, you may be ready to move to the next level with the Phase Two journal. This is a journey through the meadows where the stars walk in their dance across your sky.

Either of these paths are valid - truly neither is better nor more advanced. There is no striation or less/than better/than choice in 5D, which is where all paths we design will eventually lead you toward.

If you choose to move your studio to the Phase Two journal, I would like for you to plan to read the story of how Lisa and I developed our Phase Two relationship in conversations through Elizabeth after I left my first Miley body, and then came to live among the stars for a while. This book will be available shortly. I like working with you from the stars. When you look at the night sky your vibrational energy automatically expands and lifts. You move into your heart. It's an easy way to feel better during chaotic times. So here I am.

There is more between the words in this story, which includes the transcripts of my first few sessions speaking to Lisa and Dene through Elizabeth. These portions are living manuscripts, which means that each time you read them, the words will adjust to interact with your mind in a different way and provide new, expanded meaning. It is magic. Yes. Please allow yourself to have fun with this, and read through your heartmind.

I suggest that you only read one chapter each night. Before you go to sleep is an excellent time to read a transcript of my words, because you take so much of what you connect with then into your sleep, through the dream world into that space beyond sleep. That is where you consult with me, your own guides and others each night, sifting through what happened the previous day, as well as planning for tomorrow. You will incorporate any portions of the magic in the manuscript that you can use most directly and efficiently this way.

I am always here, in all the words you read from me in any format. Look for me through your heart, and you will feel, hear and/or see me. I am your guide, always, now. We have worked our way through this process together and your graduation cap and gown includes me by your side, now.

Postscript

This is the beginning of the stream of a new type of manifestation stream that is now actively flowing into your reality: What you are consciously creating. Now, reality created by humans can reflect humans in many ways, even in how it sometimes arrives late. You arrive late, don't you? These last pages are for recording late arrivals. Use these pages to document later arrivals as you realize the presence of your own creations surrounding you. Come back, as the reality creation scientist you are becoming, and make your notes here.

Also, know that physicality is the most dense layer of any creation and therefore the last piece to emerge and slide into place. You will shift internally, and yet up to three weeks or even more, pieces of your manifestations will still be processing and forming in the physical after you have completed this journal.

Allow that to be the case. Continue to hold your heart open in a receiving state, look for your manifestations and validate and accept them as they begin to appear, even if as a human they appear to be late on your timeline. There is no time, you see, but we will join you in joy upon your Earthly timeline when they do arrive.

There is no finish line, here. Your heart is open and what you want will grow in its flow to you.

TO CONTACT MILEY, LISA AND ELIZABETH:

Now that you have connected with Miley through this journal, she is always there for you, listening when you think of her, and providing her support to you. For a chance to connect via Elizabeth's translations with Miley, you are invited to share YOUR journaling experiences on her social media. She can be found @369Miley on Facebook, Instagram, Tiktok, and X (formerly known as Twitter).

Elizabeth and I are excited to see how all of you respond to Miley's Studio of Creation, and how Miley reponds to YOU!

To learn more about Elizabeth and interspecies communication visit her website at: CarolElizabethLong.com.

From Miley: "To subscribe to my mailing list and experience the story of Lisa's awakening now, through excerpts from our upcoming book release and more, go to 369Miley.com."

Made in the USA
Las Vegas, NV
24 September 2023

78021881R00057